UNDERSTANDING
AUTISM
SPECTRUM DISORDER

HEALTH
MATTERS

BY
HOLLY DUHIG

BookLife
PUBLISHING

©2018
BookLife Publishing
King's Lynn
Norfolk PE30 4LS

ISBN: 978-1-78637-335-9

Written by:
Holly Duhig

Edited by:
Kirsty Holmes

Designed by:
Drue Rintoul

CONTENTS

Words that look like **this** are explained in the glossary on page 31.

WHAT IS AUTISM SPECTRUM DISORDER ?

Every day we meet lots of different people and experience lots of different things. Our brains are responsible for making sense of everything we see, hear, smell, taste and feel. Autism spectrum disorder, more commonly known as autism, is the name for a whole range of **disorders** which affect how the brain does this. People with autism understand the world rather differently to others and, as a result, can find some things, like **communicating**, learning and playing, more challenging.

FACT

AROUND 1 IN EVERY 68 CHILDREN IN THE USA HAVE AUTISM SPECTRUM DISORDER.

Autism is different in every person, and the **traits** it causes can range from mild to **severe**. Because the effects of autism are a range, or spectrum, we call them autism spectrum disorders.

FACT

AUTISM AFFECTS BOTH ADULTS AND CHILDREN.

Autism is not an illness like a cold or sickness bug. Illnesses are **contagious**, which means they can be passed from person to person, and only last for a short time. Autism is not contagious and it is not something that goes away. Autism is a lifelong condition but it cannot harm you. It simply affects the way your brain interprets the world around you.

One of the main things that autism affects is the way people learn. Some people with autism might find they struggle with certain subjects at school, whereas others might find one particular subject especially interesting. People with autism often struggle with reading and writing, and many have a learning difficulty called **dyslexia**. In fact, it is thought that the famous scientist, Albert Einstein, may have had dyslexia as well as some form of autism. Einstein was especially talented at science but struggled with reading and writing.

ALBERT EINSTEIN

Autism also affects the way people **interact** with and understand other people. For people with autism, everyday conversations might be hard to follow. For example, they might find it hard to know when it's their turn to speak, when they are expected to listen to others and when they are allowed to interrupt. They might not understand other people's jokes or why they find certain things funny. All of this can make people with autism feel left out or lonely.

Over the next few pages, we will learn more about what autistic traits are and how they affect people.

AUTISM AND THE SENSES

Imagine you are at a fairground. There are lots of bright lights, music and people talking and shouting. It might be hard to hear what your friends are saying over all the other sounds and it can feel quite overwhelming. For people with autism, everyday life can feel just as overwhelming as a busy fairground. It can be hard to **filter** out the background sounds and focus on what one person is saying or doing.

Because of this, people with autism might sometimes seem unfocused, as if they are not concentrating on what you are saying. However, in reality, they are probably concentrating very hard but it's easier for them to concentrate without looking at you.

FACT

WE ALL USE FACIAL EXPRESSIONS TO SHOW HOW WE ARE FEELING. HOWEVER, PEOPLE WITH AUTISM OFTEN HAVE TROUBLE UNDERSTANDING WHAT DIFFERENT FACIAL EXPRESSIONS MEAN.

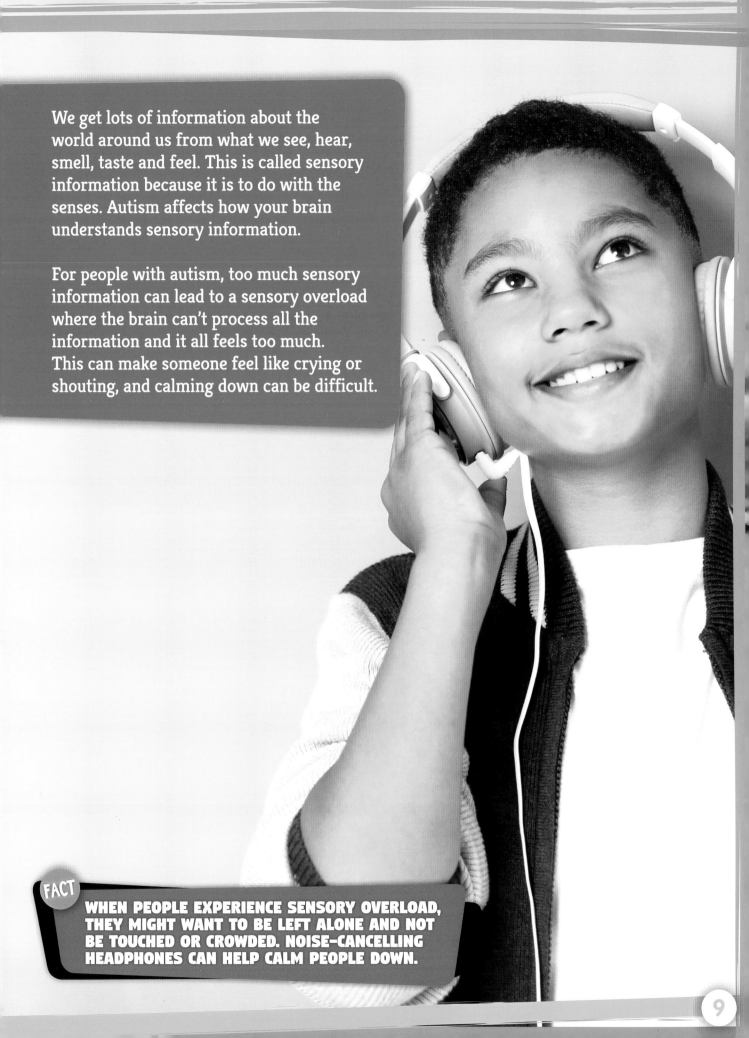

We get lots of information about the world around us from what we see, hear, smell, taste and feel. This is called sensory information because it is to do with the senses. Autism affects how your brain understands sensory information.

For people with autism, too much sensory information can lead to a sensory overload where the brain can't process all the information and it all feels too much. This can make someone feel like crying or shouting, and calming down can be difficult.

FACT

WHEN PEOPLE EXPERIENCE SENSORY OVERLOAD, THEY MIGHT WANT TO BE LEFT ALONE AND NOT BE TOUCHED OR CROWDED. NOISE-CANCELLING HEADPHONES CAN HELP CALM PEOPLE DOWN.

STIMMING

Many people with autism like to repeat certain movements or behaviours such as flapping their hands, jumping up and down, rocking, or flicking their fingers. They might even make loud noises. These actions are called 'stimming' because they are a way of **stimulating** the brain and the senses.

When sensory information feels overwhelming, stimming is a way of controlling what senses are being used and stimulated. Stimming can help people with autism to concentrate or relax, or it can simply be a habit.

Everyone has things they like to do to keep their brain busy when they're bored. Biting your nails, tapping your feet or twirling your pen are all types of stimming that give your brain something to do. For people with autism, these actions simply tend to be more noticeable and they might need to do them more often. Stimming can sometimes look frightening to people who don't understand – a person with autism might stim by banging their head or shouting. If you understand what they are doing, it isn't so scary.

People with autism often know that their stims look unusual to those around them but still find them difficult to control. This can feel very frustrating.

FIDGET CUBES, LIKE THIS ONE HERE, CAN HELP PEOPLE CONTROL THEIR STIMMING.

FACT

AUTISM MAKES IT HARD TO WORK OUT WHAT ACTIONS ARE SEEN AS USUAL AND WHAT ACTIONS ARE SEEN AS UNUSUAL IN SOCIAL SETTINGS.

AUTISM AND COMMUNICATION

Autism affects how people understand and communicate with others. To people with autism, it may seem that everyday conversation has lots of tiny details and rules that are hard to understand and remember.

VINCENT VAN GOGH'S 'THE STARRY NIGHT', 1889

Some people say that autism is a little like how it feels to be colour-blind. Colour-blind people see colours differently, and so might miss little details. Having autism might feel like this, but socially: missing out on little details in social situations that others can see.

As we grow up, we all learn the many unwritten rules of talking with other people. For example, we learn that we should talk to our teacher more politely than we would talk to our friends and that we should talk more quietly in the classroom than we would in the playground. We also learn that we have to listen to others instead of just talking about ourselves. However, for people with autism, it might be difficult or even impossible to remember these rules.

JUST LIKE IN A BOARD GAME, WE HAVE TO WAIT OUR TURN TO TALK IN CONVERSATIONS.

FACT

THE RULES OF A GAME CAN BE MEMORISED, BUT IT CAN BE HARD TO MERMORISE THE RULES OF CONVERSATIONS.

Saying What You Mean

Often in conversations people say things they don't quite mean. They might say these things to make what they are saying more interesting, or even to make people laugh. For example, someone might use the **expression** "it's raining cats and dogs" on a rainy day, but this doesn't mean animals are falling out of the sky, only that it's raining a lot. People with autism might take such expressions word-for-word and not realise when people are **exaggerating**.

DICTIONARY
OF THE ENGLISH LANGUAGE

Many people think that people with autism like to be on their own. Sometimes they do, but this is not always the case. Feeling unable to **keep up** with conversations can lead to people with autism feeling left out. Always be patient and try to include your friends with autism.

Another thing that can be difficult to understand if you have autism is sarcasm. Sarcasm is when people say the exact opposite of what they mean in order to be funny or to point out something that they think is very obvious. For example, someone might roll their eyes and say, "lovely weather we're having" even though it's raining outside. This can be confusing if you have autism.

ASPERGER SYNDROME

Asperger syndrome, sometimes called Asperger's or AS, is just one of the conditions on the autism spectrum. It is named after a **paediatrician** called Hans Asperger who worked with children who showed signs of this type of autism. AS is similar in lots of ways to other autism spectrum disorders.

For example, if you have AS, you might find understanding other people difficult. However, unlike children with other disorders on the autism spectrum, children with Asperger's normally find reading, writing and learning much easier than other people their age.

FACT

'ASPERGER' IS PRONOUNCED WITH A HARD 'G', LIKE IN 'BURGER'

Often people with AS talk using words that are very grown-up and advanced for their age. However, there is more to communication than just words. People use all sorts of things to communicate such as tone of voice, pitch, facial expression and **body language**.

For example, someone might speak in a high pitch and smile to show they are excited. If someone has Asperger syndrome, they might find it hard to understand these more complicated ways of communicating.

FACT

FOR LOTS OF PEOPLE, YAWNING IS CATCHING. IF YOUR FRIEND YAWNS, YOU ARE LIKELY TO YAWN TOO. PEOPLE WITH AUTISM ARE MUCH LESS LIKELY TO CATCH YAWNS.

SPECIAL INTERESTS

Many people with autism have special interests, which are hobbies, pastimes or topics that they find especially interesting. This is especially common for people with Asperger syndrome but people with other autism spectrum disorders have special interests too. A special interest might be about certain game, book or TV show, but often it is something more unusual such as trains or maps.

Lots of people with autism have a special interest in trains. Some experts think this is because trains have **schedules** and many people with autism like to have schedules in their day-to-day lives too.

People's special interests can be very helpful and people often turn a special interest into a **career**. For example, someone who is very interested in trains might get a job on the railways.

However, some people might get so absorbed in their special interest that they struggle to concentrate on other things, especially in school. They might not understand why others aren't as interested in their special interest as they are. They might want to talk a lot about their favourite thing but not realise that it's not the right time.

CASE STUDY: PETER

My name is Peter. I have a type of autism called Asperger Syndrome. My favourite thing to play is computer games, especially Minecraft. When I'm not playing Minecraft, I like to watch other people play it on YouTube.

My Asperger's makes talking to other people hard and sometimes boring. I like computer games because I don't have to concentrate on what other people are saying and I can play all by myself.

Mum says I'm not allowed to play computer games when we have guests because I will sometimes forget they are there and ignore them. Mum says it's rude to ignore guests. I don't mean to be rude. Mum usually sets a timer and when the alarm goes off I have to save my game and turn off the computer.

I like having things timed. It makes me feel like everything is in order. I don't like it when things take longer than they should. Luckily Mum knows how to help me stay calm when things don't go to plan!

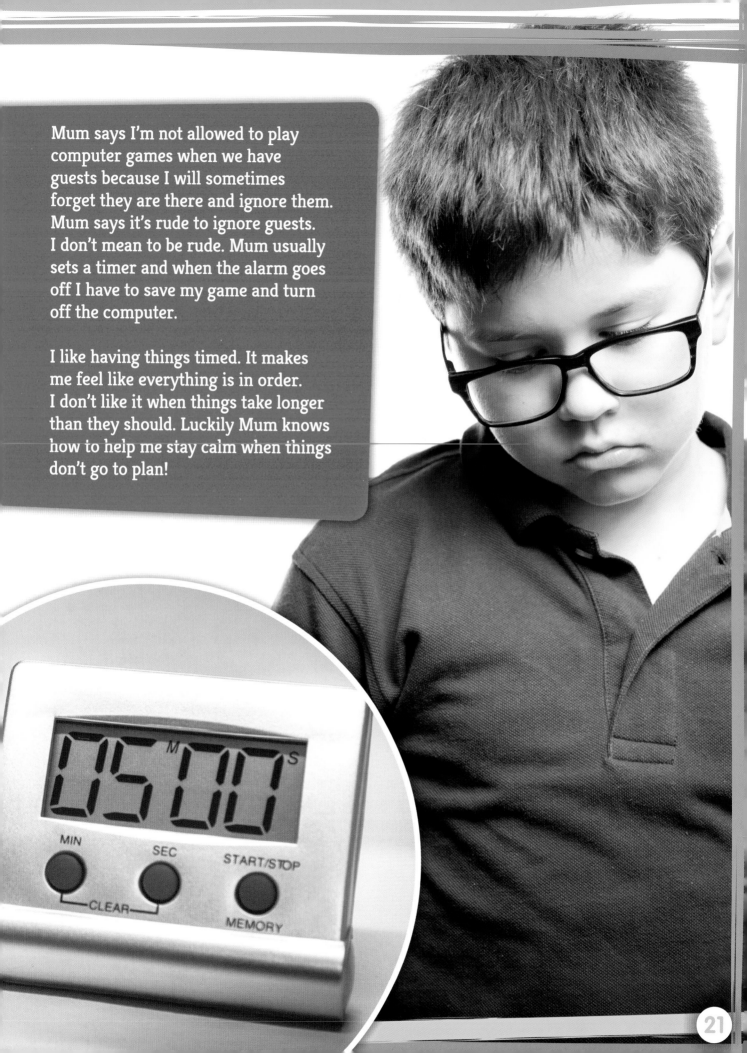

OTHER AUTISM SPECTRUM DISORDERS

PDA

Have you ever been looking forward to going to a friend's birthday party but when the day arrived you didn't want to get dressed and go? Or maybe you've been really hungry for dinner but, when someone cooked it for you, you suddenly didn't want to eat? It can be hard to understand why we do these things but, a lot of the time, it's because we feel **pressured** by people around us. When we feel pressured, we might feel anxious and want to avoid doing the things we are expected to do. This anxiety can be especially intense for people with PDA, a type of autism spectrum disorder.

Unlike people with Asperger syndrome, people with PDA struggle with time limits and schedules. They may lose track of time easily or feel stressed when given a **deadline**.

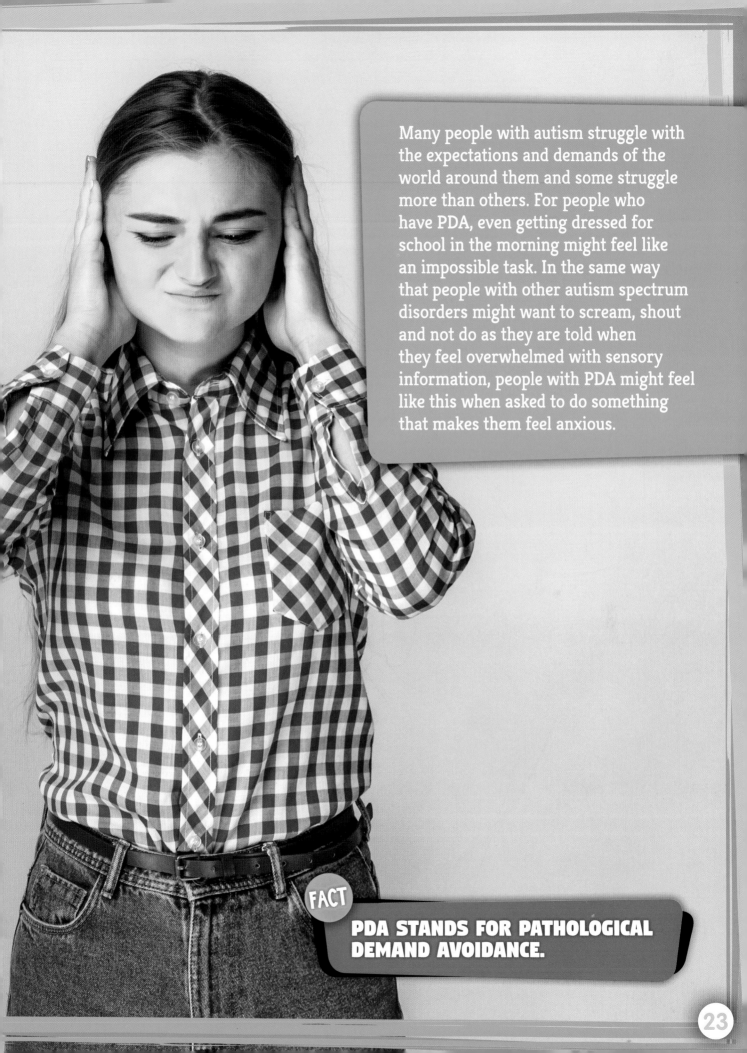

Many people with autism struggle with the expectations and demands of the world around them and some struggle more than others. For people who have PDA, even getting dressed for school in the morning might feel like an impossible task. In the same way that people with other autism spectrum disorders might want to scream, shout and not do as they are told when they feel overwhelmed with sensory information, people with PDA might feel like this when asked to do something that makes them feel anxious.

FACT

PDA STANDS FOR PATHOLOGICAL DEMAND AVOIDANCE.

CASE STUDY: ANYA

My name is Anya and I have a type of autism called PDA. Because of my PDA I like to know when things are happening and I don't like it when plans change. I often have to ask my mum over and over what time we have to leave the house to go somewhere. Keeping her answer in my head can be difficult sometimes. I have lots of thoughts going round in my head and I can get distracted very easily. I have to put all my toys away before bed otherwise I will want to play with them in the morning when I'm getting ready for school and this can make me forget to do things like put my homework in my school bag.

ON THE INSIDE OF OUR FRONT DOOR MUM HAS WRITTEN A CHECKLIST OF ALL THE THINGS I NEED TO REMEMBER TO TAKE TO SCHOOL.

Back to school
- ☐ notebook
- ☐ pencils
- ☐ pens
- ☐ ruler
- ☐ crayons

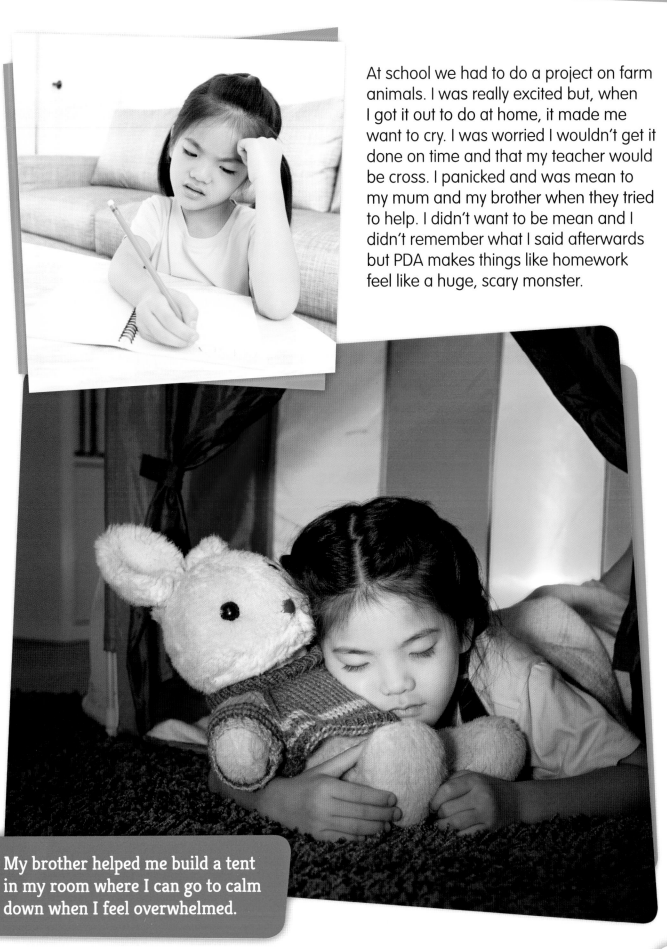

At school we had to do a project on farm animals. I was really excited but, when I got it out to do at home, it made me want to cry. I was worried I wouldn't get it done on time and that my teacher would be cross. I panicked and was mean to my mum and my brother when they tried to help. I didn't want to be mean and I didn't remember what I said afterwards but PDA makes things like homework feel like a huge, scary monster.

My brother helped me build a tent in my room where I can go to calm down when I feel overwhelmed.

AUTISM AND OTHER DISORDERS

ADHD

People with autism are also more likely to have certain conditions that are not on the autism spectrum. For example, lots of children with autism also get **diagnosed** with ADHD.

ADHD stands for attention deficit hyperactivity disorder. This is when your brain has trouble staying focused on one thing and your body has trouble keeping still. When you have autism and ADHD it can be difficult to know when it is okay to be **hyperactive** and when it is not, for example in a classroom.

FIDGET TOYS LIKE THESE CAN HELP PEOPLE WITH ADHD TO FOCUS THEIR BRAIN BECAUSE IT GIVES THEIR BODY SOMETHING TO DO.

OCD and Anxiety

Many people with an autism spectrum disorder also experience OCD. OCD stands for obsessive compulsive disorder and it is a type of anxiety disorder. It means that a person gets unwelcome thoughts (obsessions) and feels a strong need to do a movement or action (compulsion) to calm the thoughts. A trait of both autism and OCD is liking routine and getting anxious when things are changed. If this anxiety becomes so bad that it frightens you or takes up a lot of your time, it may be a sign of OCD.

FACT

AUTISM STIMS AND OCD COMPULSIONS OFTEN LOOK VERY SIMILAR AND IT IS POSSIBLE TO EXPERIENCE BOTH. THE DIFFERENCE IS THAT STIMS FEEL GOOD AND RELAXING WHEREAS COMPULSIONS ARE CAUSED BY ANXIOUS THOUGHTS.

LIVING WITH AUTISM

People with autism might need more support than others at school and even at home. Autistic traits are part of a huge spectrum and most people have some traits that are autistic. At one end of the spectrum these traits are mild. People with mild autism are often said to have a **hidden disability** because it still affects their school work, life and friendships but other people might not realise that they need extra help. Nowadays, people are more aware of autism and it is diagnosed more often so that people get the help they need.

FACT

SOME RESEARCH SHOWS THAT GIRLS ARE LESS LIKELY TO BE DIAGNOSED WITH AUTISM THAN BOYS BECAUSE THEY ARE MORE LIKELY TO HIDE AUTISTIC TRAITS. PEOPLE SHOULD NEVER HAVE TO HIDE WHO THEY ARE.

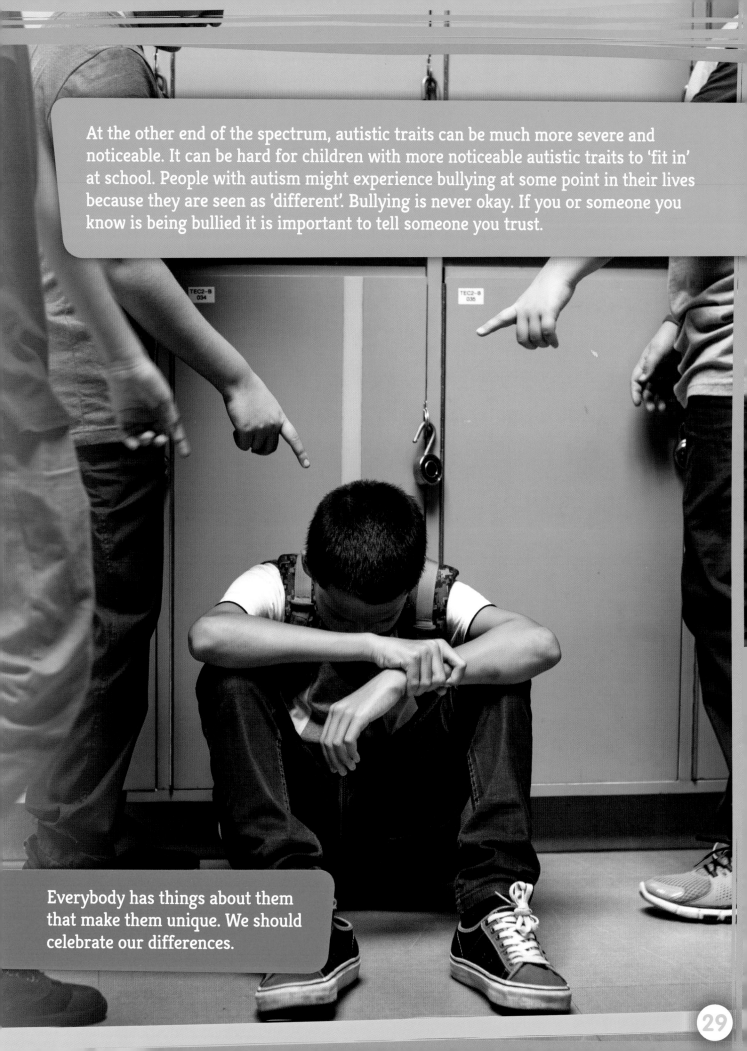

At the other end of the spectrum, autistic traits can be much more severe and noticeable. It can be hard for children with more noticeable autistic traits to 'fit in' at school. People with autism might experience bullying at some point in their lives because they are seen as 'different'. Bullying is never okay. If you or someone you know is being bullied it is important to tell someone you trust.

Everybody has things about them that make them unique. We should celebrate our differences.

In the past, autism wasn't very well understood and people who had it weren't well understood either. However, nowadays we know much more about autism and how it affects people. We now know that people with autism see the world differently to others and that this is often a good thing!

Everybody is unique and no two people with autism are the same. Learning about the things that make us different is important and can help people with conditions like autism to be understood and given the support they need.

GLOSSARY

body language	things a person does with their body that tell you how they feel
career	the job or series of jobs that you do during your working life
communicating	the passing of information between two or more people
contagious	able to be spread from person to person
deadline	a time or day by which something must be done
diagnosed	when a disease or illness has been identified by a doctor
disorder	a physical or mental sickness or ailment
dyslexia	a learning difficulty surrounding reading and words
exaggerating	distort the truth about something to make it seem greater
expression	a phrase that has a different meaning, e.g. "raining cats and dogs"
facial expressions	what a person does with their face to show emotions or reactions
filter	ignore some things and concentrate on others
hidden disability	a disability or difficulty that can't easily be seen
hyperactive	very active or stimulated
interact	responding to others socially
keep up	to understand or deal with something that is moving or changing very fast
memorised	to have committed to memory
paediatrician	a doctor who specialises in children's medicine
pressured	feeling pushed into doing something, especially if you don't want to
schedules	timetables or plans for an activity or period of time
severe	(of something bad) serious, very great or intense
social settings	somewhere people are around others, for example a party
stimulating	provoking a response
traits	qualities or characteristics of a person

INDEX

Image Credits
All images are courtesy of Shutterstock.com, unless otherwise specified. With thanks to Getty Images, Thinkstock Photo and iStockphoto.
Front Cover, 2,4,5 – Photographee.eu. 6&7 – iofoto, Anna Reznikov. 8&9 – Photomarine, Photographee.eu, Africa Studio. 10&11 – ADragan, Jeka. 12&13 – gillmar, Veja. 14&15 – PAKULA PIOTR, Photo Melon, Photographee.eu. 16&17 – Photographee.eu, Master1305, Chris Bourloton. 18&19 – Lapina, cowardlion, Albina Tiplyashina. 20&21 – antoniodiaz, luskiv, antoniodiaz, toeytoey. 22&23 – Image Point Fr, Mykola Samoilenko. 24&25 – PR Image Factory, Bridget Zawitoski. 26&27 – carballo, Mi Pan, Photographee.eu. 28&29 – Monkey Business Images, Rawpixel.com. 30 – Photographee.eu.